DO NOT GET BETWEEN A
WOMAN and her CHOCOLATE

Some harsh realities that the Male of the species has to understand when dealing with the wonders of a woman.

Marcus Tempus

ACKNOWLEDGMENTS

When the idea for this book came into my head I just happened to be meeting two friends, Beverley and Anastasia. They thought it was a great idea provided they took over editorial control.

My pen but ladies in control.

Please blame them if you read anything that you do not like.

Nothing changes, it is never a man's fault!

I would also like to thank the many women that discussed this subject with me during the research for the book. Your pleasure and help in discussing two of your favorite subjects, SEX and Chocolate, is noted with thanks and appreciation.

DON'T GET BETWEEN A WOMAN AND HER CHOCOLATE

This book started as one of those 20 second elevator conversations in down town Chicago. I joined a couple of ladies engrossed in a discussion.

I smiled said "hello," they said "sorry just talking about a chocolate cake."

I replied "no problem, never get between a woman and chocolate." They laughed.

I went on and said "It is the biggest shock for a man to have to come to terms with. Gradually being replaced in a woman's affections by children her friends and then ultimately chocolate."

They laughed and replied, "Yes, and it doesn't take that long either." I agreed. The door opened, we all left.

As is so often the case some casual comments and bonding laughter masks some basic observations, "that ring true."

So I thought it is worth a book about how a man has to come to terms with the evolution of the relationships with the women in his life. How the many phases of a woman's life impact a man and interacts with the many phases of a man's life.

Then for a man to finally recognize that chocolate may be more important than him. A nonsensical thought at one level, but the evidence to support this theory is a bit scary.

When I started writing this book it was intended as a bit of fun, tongue in cheek. This has however turned out to be a huge learning experience. My research has wandered into some interesting issues. It is very clear that some women see Chocolate as more than pleasure. Chocolate can also mean independence and control.

Men, you could learn a lot from what I have found out about women and their love for chocolate, and yes most of the women that I spoke to preferred Chocolate to SEX.

I hope that you enjoy?

INDEX

FACTS, FIGURES, STATISTICS, OPINIONS AND PREJUDICES

Before you embark on reading this book a few words about the information that it contains and where the many numbers and survey information quoted has originated from.

All of the information and quotes used have been taken from somewhere and have not been made up. They typically have come from a small survey group and I have either read them or heard them on a serious media program.

The personal research involving over 60 women I can vouch for as being entirely accurate and it has been faithfully reported. Some of the comments are based upon a very small sample, often of one, which I may well have used to relay an opinion that I thought was interesting or significant and could probably apply to a lot of other people.

I have tried to use some judgement and common sense, based of course upon my own male bias. I have only tried to use information that I broadly believe to be indicative of the point that I am trying to make.

This is not a book prepared by psychiatrists, or academics or people studying the behavior of rats, pigeons and dogs. The book is about life as the editorial team have experienced it, and as the 61 women that took part in the research have told us.

I do not believe that there is a single "Indisputable totally accurate Fact" in the book. Even the statistical research that has been used which has a numerate conclusion is questionable. For example one piece of research that I read concluded that 84% of women have at some time had sex just for a quiet life. Not 80% or 90% mind, 84%. Even a very basic study of statistical sampling indicates that in any sample the outcome will have a tolerance or range of outcomes depending upon the size of the sample, the total population and the sampling technique used.

You can draw your own conclusion as to the range of the answer for a total population of several hundred million women with a sample maybe a few thousand. In my view a result in the order of 84% would be termed " nearly all women" but I quote the 84% because that was the research outcome.

All of these various pieces of research are largely opinions, or come from a very small sample group, which can often be discredited. There is nearly always an alternative point of view. I have therefore used my highly developed set of male opinions and prejudices to select the theories that make my point. In the event that I may over step the mark, and a dubious comment ends up in print, this will be entirely due to the two ladies that are checking this book.

You may be expecting to see many footnotes all referenced in a section at the back of the book. Well that could be the first disappointment when reading this book.

The English language has some interesting nuances. What we say and what people hear are not always the same. A word or two about some of the words that are used in this book and how I have tried to use them correctly.

"Most." This word means more than half, or over 50% and I have used it quite a lot to make that very precise point. It is a word that can be very misleading. For example a few years back a UK government minister said that "Most" eggs had the salmonella virus. When she (note) made that comment she had read some research that I think indicated that the outer shell in 50 to 60 % of eggs had shown microscopic traces of Salmonella.

Her point, given this research, was entirely accurate, but maybe mis-leading? The problem was that what people heard was not most but "Nearly All" if not every single egg was now carrying the virus, actually in the egg. A massive national political row ensued.

"Most" therefore means more than 50%. If I think a point applies to more than say 80% of the population then I use the word " Nearly all". The word "Typically" will mean that for "Most" people that is the expected behavior. "Many" will mean a significant amount but probably not "Most" and "Some" will mean that sufficient women (less than "most") behave like this to make a point that I believe you should be aware of. I have tried to use these terms consistently as defined.

The book has also been checked and edited by two very experienced "Women of the World." Between us we know a lot of stuff and if we think that any of the research is suspect or misleading it has been changed or removed. We have also on a few occasions used our own theories (posh name for an opinion).

Above all this is a book intended to take a light hearted look at one particular aspect of human behavior. There are some serious points in the book but please take the book with a "pinch of salt." Always remember there are very few absolute certainties in human behavior, We are all different and it is up to you to manage your life in a way "That works for you."

"Uncertainty is not a pleasant condition. But certainty is absurd."
Voltaire circa 1790

WHAT EXACTLY IS
CHOCOLATE?

Chocolate is a food stuff derived from the cocoa bean. It contains some seriously bad stuff, fat and sugars. The number of calories in all types of chocolate is approximately 500 per 100g (3.5 ounces). Therefore a one pound box of chocolates contains approximately 2200 calories. The recommended daily intake for a healthy diet for women is 1900 calories per day or the equivalent of just under one pound box of chocolates. A bar of chocolate is typically 500 calories or just over 25% of the recommended food intake.

Dark chocolate is considered to be best because even though it has the same amount of calories as milk chocolate it also contains some good stuff depending upon the % cocoa. A good bar would have 70% or more cocoa.

One of the most pleasant effects of eating chocolate is the "good feeling" that many people experience after indulging. Chocolate contains more than 300 known chemicals. Scientists have been working on isolating specific chemicals and chemical combinations which may explain some of the pleasurable effects of consuming chocolate. Opinions still differ on what is actually in chocolate.

Caffeine is the most well known of these chemical ingredients, and while it may be present in chocolate, it can only be found in small quantities. Theobromine, a weak stimulant, is also present in slightly higher amounts. The combination of these two chemicals (and possibly others) may provide the "lift" that chocolate eaters experience.

Scientific opinion is divided on the presence of caffeine and some scientists believe that chocolate does not contain it and that Theobromine is the main active ingredient in chocolate (1 to 3%) it only occurs in cacao which comes from the chocolate bean. These are some of its properties;

mild effect

very slow onset

long lasting

50% in bloodstream after 6 to 10 hrs

increases feeling of well being

mild antidepressant

gentle, smooth, sensual stimulation

stimulates cardiovascular system

stimulates muscular system

mild effect on central nervous system

almost no one is allergic

not addictive

no withdrawal symptoms

mild diuretic

stimulates the kidneys

A pretty good bunch of properties that could create the main reason why chocolate is eaten. Theobromine is a strong stimulant and was used by the Spanish to keep their armies going while conquering Central and South America.

Chocolate (real Chocolate, not candy) can keep you up at night, especially in very young children (but that doesn't mean that it includes caffeine). Nursing mothers who eat pure chocolate may also find their children happy and wide awake several hours later.

There are several minor psychoactive chemicals in Chocolate. Theo-bromine: Phenylethylamine, Theophylline, Tele-methylhistamine Phenyethyl-amine, affects mood swings by causing an initial emotional high then a short time later an emotional low. It causes blood pressure and blood-sugar levels to rise, resulting in a feeling of alertness and contentment.

Chocolate is believed by some to contain Caffeine because it has the same structure as Theobromine but there is no analytical evidence to sup-port this. Just to contrast the two these are the properties of caffeine;

intense
strong effect
fast acting
rapid dissipation
50% in bloodstream after 2 to 5 hrs
increases alertness
increases emotional stress
jagged, nervous stimulation
stimulates cardiovascular system
stimulates respiratory system
strong effect on central nervous system
many people allergic
physically addictive
many proven withdrawal symptoms
extreme diuretic
requires large intake of fluids to balance the diuretic effect

There are a number of serious health problems associated with caffeine, most of which have not been associated with Theobromine:

Large quantities of Caffeine have shown decreased sperm counts in rats. (So please do not mate with a RAT!)

Well controlled studies have suggested that 2% of miscarriages could be due to Caffeine in coffee. Dehydration headaches. Most headaches (estimates range from 50% to 90%) are caused by dehydration, and one of the primary causes of dehydration in the USA is the large quantity of Caffeine that most people consume. (Caffeine laden drinks like CocaCola and Coffee don't quench your thirst, they actually increase it!). Caffeine can also be associated with heart trouble and stress. Chocolate is therefore a better fix for the body than say Coffee.

Dark Chocolate. Research conducted by the University of California revealed that dark chocolate has several health benefits. This type of chocolate contains flavonoids, which are naturally occurring chemicals that increase nitric oxide levels in the blood. This promotes better blood flow and relaxation of the arteries. In addition, the relaxed feeling that occurs after eating a piece of dark chocolate was found to occur because dark chocolate can raise serotonin levels in the brain. Dark chocolate also contains antioxidants, which neutralize free radicals and slow down the destruction of cells.

One recent study in the UK concluded that 100g of dark chocolate with 60 to 70% cocoa content taken by 2000 people with a high risk of having a heart attack or stroke indicated that it may reduce the number of fatal attacks by 15 and semi fatal attacks by 70 per 10,000 people. This was considered to be due to the presence of "Flavonoids." The researchers even went so far as to recommend that it should be prescribed free at a cost of $35 per year, per person, to supply a 100g bar of dark chocolate daily. Guess what? This treatment has few side effects and a high level of compliance. Sceptics say that the benefits are off set by the higher calorific value. There is a term for this conflict.

Cognitive Dissonance. This is where two or more of your basic beliefs are in conflict with each other. For example If you've ever felt the need to tell a lie and was uncomfortable because you see yourself as scrupulously honest, then you've experienced cognitive dissonance. It occurs whenever your view of yourself clashes with your performance in any area. This has to be a factor in eating chocolate. You know that it is not good for you as a food because of the high calorie content. But you believe that it contains certain compounds that are good for you so you still eat it. I did read up on this quite a bit and have only one take away that I will mention about "Cognitive dissonance." It can be a great opportunity for mental growth coming to terms with the reality of having to deal with this inner conflict of values. Maybe that's one of the many reasons why women eat chocolate, to develop their psychological strength?

I will digress slightly to show you a little insight into the male mind. I only recently was made aware of the term "Cognitive Dissonance" having heard it in the movie "Midnight in Paris." So I looked it up. I think that I have used it correctly. I thought it would look good in this book, but I am still unable to pronounce it correctly.

Men are simple egocentric show-offs at heart. Thought that you should know, it may help. To contrast that simple thought with a more complex one. The actor that plays Ernest Hemingway in the " Midnight in Paris" film talks to Owen Wilson in the back of a car about how making love to a truly great women can create a brief moment of immortality. I would recommend every man to read this dialogue, mark and learn.

A study at Harvard University found that people who eat chocolate three times a month may live almost a year longer than those who don't. Before you get too excited, it also found that people who eat too much chocolate have a lower life expectancy. This is linked to the incidence of obesity through the higher fat and sugar consumption.

A WOMAN.

I am an object to most of you.
Not caring what I do
My thoughts and dreams
No interest to you
Something to own you think
Hit me, do me, is how you see
What you want from me
Not a friend to talk to
Gently make love to.
Listen to and try to see.
My thoughts are not the same as yours
You should enjoy them all the same
Not just remember my name
Respect is all I ask from you
Appreciate that I am different
In everything I do.
I have emotions that change
They create intrigue for you to enjoy
Don't always act like a small boy.
If one day, I say
"I have had enough, good bye
I am going my way."
Don't be surprised at what you hear
If you have created that thought
For many a year.

THE AGES OF
WOMEN

This section attempts to explain how a man experiences
the many aspects of a woman through out their life.

"People discuss my art and pretend to understand as if it were
necessary to understand, when it's simply necessary to love."

Claude Monet

MOMMY

An undisputed fact is that the first woman that a man comes into contact with is his "Mom." A relationship that can last for a very longtime and one that can help shape the man that he becomes. Sometimes, tragically, it may last for a brief moment if you are given away or, regrettably, your mother does not make it through the process of bringing you into this world.

For most men those early years help to form how they develop and what their attitude to woman will become. Guess what one of the key factors will be? Right;

The experiences and opinions your mother has formed of men through her own life and experiences.

Men should hope that their dad and other men have done a good job for the male species.

After a man is born, for those few early critical years his mother has the most intimate experience with this boy. This child will grow up to become a man. It may well be that he does not have a similar level of intimacy with another woman for quite some time, if ever.

During these early intimate years he will probably get to be breast fed. His mother will also clear up all those horrible liquids that as a baby the boy will emit from every orifice, sometimes without warning. This is very early programing, conditioning, into how the man will behave if he ever grows up, which many men actually get to do.

In those early years the man's emotions are raw and not very well developed, but very effective. A lesson that is not usually taken by the man into later life. A grown man will typically mask or hide his emotions. For example, if as a child he is hungry and starts to cry then he will usually get fed straight away by mommy. In later life, to see lines of grown men crying outside a restaurant waiting to be fed is not a good long term game plan.

Why does this early conditioning as a baby not equate in the mind of a man, that a show of emotions result in a woman providing what they need? Interesting question for the psychiatrists.

At some point most men evolve into more mature human beings, but some men like to keep some child like qualities as they believe that a woman may find this attractive. Of course the child-like qualities that a man chooses to keep will make a big difference as to how the results from this course of action may play out. Personally, I like the breast dependency coupled with having a woman doing everything for you. I suspect many men would agree. Men are primeval creatures at the core.

There is quite a substantial amount of good research indicating that how a mother brings a child up in those critical first five years can have a pretty dramatic effect on a man's behavior in two areas. Men may try and replace their mother with another woman who provides the care and support that she did. The other behavioral point is a little more convoluted. Men may treat women badly as a way of getting back at their mother because she was possibly too dominant, when the man was a child, and the man resented it.

The other major contribution that mothers make is to condition men to the powers of chocolate. Guess what every little boy is encouraged to buy his mother? A box of chocolates. I was discussing this point with one of the women research contributors and she said its even worse than that. As a child she was encouraged by her mother to eat the whole chocolate Easter bunny in one bite, head included, not even just its ears. Men would never come up with that one. Maybe?

When I was doing the research for this book I asked several woman what the one piece of advice that they would give a man to help them to better relate to a women. Several women said a man should show more of his feminine side, one woman even said that a man should become gay! Many women like gay men and have them as valuable friends. A gay man is often on the same wave length and understands them. They will shop with them and will talk for hours about relationships. Yet another quirk of fate that men have to deal with. The men that often get on best with a woman happen to be gay.

This outcome led me to think about a very basic question, male logic and all that. Women understand that a man showing his feminine side is appreciated by women and that this will enable a man to relate to, and deal better with a women. So why does a mother not embark on any form of train-ing or coaching in this area for her son? who happens to be a baby man and in some cases actually grows up to become a real grownup man with all these insensitivities? So why is that?

I have asked several men that question and I also remember from my early experiences that this does not usually happen. In fact the exact opposite is usually true. Boys are encouraged by mom to be boys. A mom will often have the fear of creating " A mommy's boy " therefore "Dad" is often deployed to develop all those manly insensitive traits in the young boy to toughen him up. Strange? I am pretty sure that women do not connect the dots and realize that a son becomes a man and how he is developed in those early years under the control of mom will greatly influence the outcome of how he will ultimately relate to and deal with women. Reap as you sow!

A mommy's boy by the way can be a huge problem for a father. Of course the more obvious situation of having to share the affections of the woman in your life, his mom. A more practical problem is starting to develop in these difficult economic times. Children are finding it increasingly more difficult to find a job and make their own way in the world. They stay at home. Guess what type of boy will prefer to do this and not want to go out in the big bad world and find out what it is all about? Right, a "mommy's boy." He may be stuck with mom (and the man, "Dad," consequently) for a longtime. This was not usually part of the original script when deciding to have children way back, when it seemed a good idea.

I do recall as a teenager having a friend that was raised by his mom as a single parent. She seriously developed his feminine side. He used to go to bed every night with face cream on and he regularly used hand cream. His skin was a lovely shade of pure white.

A visit to his apartment with mom present was always amusing to us testosterone charged teenagers, watching the hugging and kissing. You can imagine that he was constantly ridiculed by all of us, his school mates. This is the real kicker. When ever we were in the company of girls, or at a party, he usually got the best girl, easily and quickly. Even then all of us men missed the clues.

Moms rarely train a son to be aware of his feminine side and to do household chores. Two of the major complaints women have about men is that men do not show their feminine side and they are useless in the home and do not help. In the last two sentences are two huge, very difficult to find, clues as to what a possible way ahead could be. Do you get them? Moms are women. Sons become men. (Not rocket science.)

A mom question then. "Why are you not training your sons to become the type of emotionally sensitive type of man that women will relate to?" Or if that is maybe too much. Why do you not train your sons to do simple tasks required to live in a house alone, like; cooking, washing, grocery shopping, cleaning etc. I see this a major failing in a lot of woman by not creating a fully trained and sensitized man.

The concluding thoughts for this section. If you do not like the way a man behaves it is probably due to the influence of another woman "His Mother." Maybe helped by his sisters. If you do not like anything that you read in this book, this is not my problem, it has been edited by two other women. In short, nothing is my fault.

You are seeing a highly developed example of the male species reverting exactly to type. Nothing to do with me and any problems are usually caused by women.

Wonderful. Read on it gets better.

SCHOOL AND THE EARLY YEARS.

This is the period when the man is still a boy and probably will be living at home under some form of parental control, guidance and economic support. Normally this will last until the mid teens when the boy leaves the nest to make his way in the world. He returns for the good stuff. Money, food and free lodgings. There have been recorded instances of this period lasting for some men well past the teenage years.

For many men this time is when they first meet "girls" and realize that they are strange and different creatures. They look different, have different body parts and they giggle a lot. This is usually done in a huddle when they are talking about some boring things. Men realize that girls are not the same as them fairly quickly. This process can be accelerated if the man has a sister.

The family unit is the first classroom for men to be trained on the wonders and joys of women. As with all classroom learning situations the other people in the class will make a difference. This is just as true with the outcome of a boy in the different family class sizes and their composition. A boy with just a mommy and daddy to look after him will have a hugely different experience than the boy that is the fifth born with four elder sisters. Hell or nirvana, it could be either.

A man will develop attitudes and responses to women dependent upon the number of sisters that he has, where he is in the birth sequence and the age spread between the children. All or any of these factors can make a huge difference to the type of man that emerges from the "Family Classroom." Another clue just to show you where we are going, sisters are women. These interchangeable words that all end up with one of the two sexes.

During these early years the boy learns that women come in different shapes and sizes and they have different roles; mother, daughter, sister, friend, grandmother, aunt, cousin, each one of these roles requiring the women to play a different part.

The only role left for a man to experience is to have a woman as an intimate partner to confide in, have sex with, and if you are really lucky, to fall deeply in love with. Not necessarily in that order! These joys of intimacy normally have to wait for a while. I do not count the "I will show you mine, if you show me yours," game which six-year-olds may play. Mind you the evolution of the species is resulting in young people experiencing sexual intimacy at an increasingly earlier age.

Modern communications and the internet pose a huge threat to the development of young boys. Explicit porn is readily available and young minds with no emotional content or strong parental influence will get a totally distorted view of women. These readily obtainable images in no way provide a positive image of women. The porn industry is huge and I think it has a major impact on the way some men treat women. Porn films are largely there for one purpose. If I tell you that the porn films in hotel rooms are usually watched for an average of 12 minutes you can figure out what the purpose may be.

Porn films are watched by most men at some time in their lives and for some men throughout their sexually active lives. This hidden, rarely talked about (well not in polite circles) industry must have an impact of the way some men view and treat women.

A really depressing and worrying example is the recent case in the UK of a 12 year old boy attacking his 9 year old next door neighbor after watching porn. He told the police that as a result of watching the porn he "wanted to feel grown up." That little box in the house is bringing some serious behavior changes into "some" very young and immature heads.

The other lesson learned in this early classroom is that women behave differently in certain situations than men. They also use some other forms of behavior to get what they want. Enter Emotions! The start of a life long lesson with no concluding graduation. The mystery begins. The young boy starts to witness some early signs of the female of the species at work; crying.

These early years are a learning experience about the many joys and moods of young women. Men have a great advantage because these young women are just as curious as the men. Neither sex knowing enough to provide generic classifications of the other. Differences are a joy, and lets face it for most men, and a lot of women, it is all about sexual experimentation and adventure. Emotional development is crude and primitive and how we turn out is often a matter of luck. Especially if we avoid two potentially life long reminders, unwanted children and some STDs. (Sexually transmitted diseases)

FALLING IN LOVE. THE FORMATIVE PERIOD

This is usually when a man is in the mid- teens and maybe has left the nest to make his way in the world. A period of self discovery essentially helped by the relationships that he will start to form outside the family unit, especially with women.

Men often wander through those early fumbling years of experimentation without the wisdom of experience. Not realizing that "Lets do it" is maybe not the best foreplay or not appreciating the two year rule. For the uninitiated the two year rule goes something like this.

Most people in these heady years "Fall in Love" as a result of raging hormones and magic, this is a great and exciting experience. As with all great and exciting experiences it does not last. The research varies slightly but some where between one and two years the so called magic or chemistry will go in most relationships. When this happens we have to make a choice. Do we like this other person enough to want to be with them and work on making the relationship work, or not? When we are young and driven by these basic urges men frequently just recycle women because it is more fun. The recycling period can often be reduced to well below 2 years. Sometimes just 24 hours. Maybe even less!

When I was a young man the hot film was "The Graduate." I just looked it up, 1967. Was it really that long ago? Many young men aspired to be Benjamin and were looking for a Mrs. Robinson" to provide some sexual initiation or excitement. I suspect this does happen but personally I do not know anyone that has experienced a Mrs. Robinson event. In today's parlance, of course, this Mrs. Robinson effect is called "MILF" one of the many derogatory / complimenting terms young men use at this early informative stage to describe women.

Most of the descriptive terms directed at women by men relates to them as a sex object, someone to be conquered. With some of this early language I do have a problem like the concept of wanting "To Do" or "Bang" a woman a term regularly used by a lot men. "I would do her in a heart beat " is a common descriptive term men use to describe a woman. This being the ultimate accolade for a woman and meaning, "I am prepared to have sex with you." Very primitive.

When a man takes the high ground of sensitivity it is a surprise to hear his loved one come out with these terms like "I am just so ready to be done today." This can be very confusing when women talk dirty and you are trying to protect their dignity with more respectful language. So why?

Well of course I have a theory and it is in two parts. Part one is that I believe woman are much more sexually basic in a lot of instances than men appreciate. It can be a scary and very educating experience to overhear a group of women talking about their sex lives. Part two is that when a woman is in a relationship, two very important factors are usually present, commitment and trust. The woman will relax and within reason anything goes. The difference between the sexes being that for a woman this type of language is relationship specific. For a man it is their normal behavior. Just an opinion.

The other really bad aspect of falling in love for men is that men are usually no where near mature enough or emotionally evolved that they can make these, often life changing, decisions at this early time in their life. Men are very much taking a ticket in a lottery. This is evidenced by the fact that nearly 50% of marriages and long term relationships fail.

Here I also have to agree with what so many women think. Men use their penis as a brain. But typical of women they use this fact to their advantage to get men into a relationship and then complain later on when it doesn't suit them.

Some men do attempt to try and work out what love is and how they maybe are afflicted. Asking those key questions. Is she the one? Are we soul mates? Do I just love you or am I in love with you? Men do not really have any where sensible to go for answers, except the movies. All round them they will see examples of every type of relationship working, or not working with no apparent logic as to why. Wise council will say things like. You will know! It will feel right! Not very helpful to the confused young man. Yet totally meaningful for the experienced man of the world. Yet another example of men being built the wrong way round. I am starting to form the opinion that if men lived their lives backwards they would be far more attractive to women. Maybe?

Men often drift along in this happy state of ignorance until a woman traps them. Sometimes women are even more devious and hook men, in this hormone charged period, without explaining what the future holds. Forgetting to provide some essential information like, just how much hard work it is going to be to keep the relationship going. Many woman will have a plan, all worked out in their head, for the life they wish to lead. The man just happens to be signed on to play one of the parts.

Some men *do* however escape and stay in this continual cycle with women of "meet, enjoy then leave" for a longtime. Are these the heroes in the eyes of many men? Well actually no, they are usually, for some unknown reason, often pretty sad men. A serious relationship with a women does seem to have a grounding impact on a man.

Getting married is a classic example, where women quite cruelly take advantage of this weakness. Men are going along in this hormone charged bliss and then "wow" before they know what hit them, it has happened, the man is in a relationship. Women use their sexual favors to totally distort a man's thinking. A woman knows the way to get a man. They know that a man will *do* virtually anything if they keep him satisfied sexually as this will temporally park the brain function.

Men during this often idyllic time miss the clues, the little pieces of bad behavior, the way women maybe talk to our friends, the nasty comments women make about people that we laugh at because we are inside the situation. Sex is in and objectivity is out. What a powerful weapon women have. They use in a cunning and often devious manner. No wonder men have no chance.

THE COMMITMENT.

Somewhere along the way this happy free wheeling love affair starts to become institutionalized into a steady relationship, a permanent relationship, a long term relationship. Maybe marriage.

I know the little secret about woman. They control most of what goes on in a relationship, men are just victims that are often given the illusion of being in control by the woman. So many of the "big decisions" in a relationship are driven by the woman. There are two very good reasons for this. First women are usually better at it. Second it makes life easier for most men for women to take over.

When men are considering this long-term opportunity to sail off into the sunset they are often under the control of a strong emotional persona and their more basic instincts. Or as so many women often succinctly put it "Our penis is doing the thinking." Rational thought seems to go out the window at the time of decision. This is probably a good idea for most men. They will probably receive good advice often from other married men, which they will of course totally ignore. For example, have a look at their mother because in 20 years or so that's what you will be dealing with? Good or bad? Men will also ignore all the little warning signs about behavior because when they are with their loved, one men believe that it will be different for them.

Trust me if you have a problem in this idyllic hormone charged phase of a relationship then a long term commitment is unlikely to correct the problem and will usually make it worse. If there are any difficult areas of compatibility then those problems will be magnified as a result of spending more time together. The good stuff becomes taken for granted and the bad stuff gets magnified. Hence the expression "you never know what you have until its gone" which only applies to the good stuff of course.

The graduation event for this formative relationship building period is the entry into a long term relationship, usually marriage. Unfortunately the course work, unlike most colleges, does not prepare a man for the institution that he is about to graduate into. Premature graduation is not uncommon and can lead to many years of collective misery for all concerned. This is one graduation that an early pass may not always be the wisest thing to do. A couple of early failures, maybe the odd resit could be good character building stuff. As one of my teachers used to say when we were having trouble grasping a point "You are staying in until you get it right." Good advice on so many levels. These things should not be rushed. Men should take their time about when to graduate and with who of course.

WHERE DID MY LOVER GO?

Men start in this lovely relationship with a wonderful woman, if they are lucky? Life is great, they move round, go places, live in the now, make love as frequently as they chose and all is well in the world. Then maybe our biological programming kicks in, or more likely the woman's biological clock kicks in, and men feel so good about this wonderful relationship that they may wish to immortalize it with the creation of a child. What a joy, what a great idea, this will be the first of many. A large happy family. Perfect!

Most of the people who think like this have had no actual experience of raising children to validate that view. Yet still they do it. The benefits of having children is not a clear cut case. There are many good and serious arguments why bringing children into some relationships may not be a good idea. Some people are just not programmed to be parents. But here we have logic, common sense and a load of experience stacked up against hormones, biological programming and emotions. A totally uneven contest. Hello babies. Unfortunately life has to be experienced and usually cannot be taught.

Let me quickly add that family life is great and it provides fulfilment and satisfaction for billions of people on this planet and I would not have it any other way. But it is not all smooth sailing and all men should be prepared for some difficult issues. Not everyone is suited to raise a family or have been lucky enough to be in the right situation for the raising of a family to be possible.

The first issue to deal with when a baby arrives is that the man is usually replaced as the number one love of their partner's life by a child. Your lover has gone, at least temporally and in some case forever. Women are strange creatures. Giving birth to a child can screw up their hormones and most of them develop a completely different attitude to sex and all the good stuff that men enjoy.

This always happens. If you are lucky it could be for a very short period, a matter of weeks, until the body recovers. It could however last until the children have left home when the woman may then develop a whole new sexual persona.

If you are really unlucky, the woman may never be the same again and she will lose all interest in sex, and that certainly happens. It does sort of make sense as I believe that we are the only animal species that has sex for pleasure. There must be some members of our species that are at the more basic level and once they have produced an offspring the job is done so the mating urges dissipate. I have absolutely no evidence to back this up, but it does make some kind of sense.

On the extremely positive side, I have heard that some women actually have an enhanced sex drive after pregnancy and they find the experience releasing and it opens up a more vibrant and sensuous woman. I think that this could be one of those " Urban myths" spread by women to fool men.

When the children arrive, they not only change the emotional priorities for a women but they could also affect her physically. She may well be tired most of the time which could last for years especially if she works and has other children. Her body will change, maybe forever. Not every women is disciplined enough to work out in order to return to their former shape. Those beautiful breasts that you have enjoyed could have literally been milked dry to become a shadow of their former selves.

Freedom of action becomes seriously curtailed, no more just popping out for a quick meal on an impulse. Baby sitters will be required, feeding times have to be taken into account. Traveling becomes a nightmare, loads of stuff to take and you become anti social at so many levels with this noisy little person disrupting the peace and tranquility for so many other people.

When you decide to produce children you are taking a huge gamble. Your lover will have gone, and her sex drive will definitely change. It is just a question of for how long and how will she return? You will now be sharing the affections of your lover with a child. This could of course not only effect your relationship with your lover but also with the child. Hopefully it will be a loving and joint exercise. Make sure that it is raised to the best of your ability. After all sex is not that important. Well, maybe not to the woman in your life, as many of them can get by with more chocolate.

Having a child can be hugely rewarding but it is high risk and will change your life. So think it through. Then do it anyway! No one is going to listen to all this really good and accurate advice. Save it for the "I now know what you mean" day.

CHILDREN ARE FOREVER.

A child, the embodiment of us, the ultimate we can create on this planet. Our pride and joy and a whole new person upon which to focus our love, joy, affection and usually a considerable amount of money. Ok so that's all probably true for most people. Now it is time for a few realities;

A touching conversation I quite often hear is a couple with a young family starting a sentence with the expression "When the kids have gone." Guess what? "They are never gone! "They just change their personalities, grow up and become more expensive. Luckily, the only constant with children is that they usually always need money. So that is great. At least it is a way of getting to see them on a regular basis.

Raising children should be looked at in four phases.

Phase one is the birth and baby phase, you just have this smelly little creature that has to be fed and cleaned until this baby starts to do some-thing interesting like walk or talk.

Phase two is maybe the best phase when you realize that you have a little person to influence, train, look after and impress. They will view you as a god almost regardless of the job that you do bringing them up as they know no better.

This period usually lasts into the early teenage years if you are lucky. It is however getting shorter with the stimulus of the modern media.

Phase three is the teenage years where quite frankly you just cross your fingers and hope for the best. You could have a multi-personality nightmare, or a sullen non-communicative eating machine or maybe a normal teenager, whatever that is? Or you may have all of these in any one week. This is a really critical time in a child's life as they are having to experience some significant biological changes and to adjust to the world outside.

Bad experiences in these teenage years have been known to destroy family units and marriages in extreme cases. Much of what happens to the teenager in phase three are unknown to parents who are usually on a need to know basis by the child. Which is a surprisingly better idea than you may think.

Phase 4. The child is a young adult and hopefully leaves the family home to find their way in the world, maybe a job or college. With a bit of luck this will mean they have left home for good only to return as, hopefully welcome, visitors.

When they leave you should immediately rent their room out or convert it to some purpose that renders it uninhabitable. If the teenage years have a been a really bad experience, move to another home and do not tell them.

For the lucky parents, the children go off and form relationships, develop a life of their own and treat their parents with respect and as friends. Returning once in a while to supply gifts and to demonstrate their many collective and creative ways of asking for money. Houses, cars, insurances etc.

Ideally this huge investment of time and money coupled with all the emotional changes that you have endured as parents will give some payback. You wish?

I have tried to discuss this with my grown up children. When I discuss the issues I try and keep it professional and of course financial so I use the "Sinking Fund Argument" being a smart ass. It goes something like this.

So kids, we have done a great job bringing you up, and you all have jobs doing great in the world (hope they are?) I wondered what you were doing to look after us when the time comes, as a sort of pay back. I suggest that you all get together and open an account, some form of "Sinking Fund," to which you all contribute. When we are older and in need of help then you will be able to use this fund to look after us in our golden years. After all, it's only fair, the circle of life etc. Must be a good idea.

I do not normally get all of this speech out and still retain their interest or even their presence? I could be speaking Chinese as judged by their reaction.

Then guess what these lovely children may actually then go out and breed. You may have to go through some of all this stuff again. Luckily you can often just get the best out of the grandchildren and be super grandparents and leave the mucky and tiring stuff to their mom, or maybe dad as well. If you have trained him well?

WHO AM I?

The arrival of Children brings many joys and pleasures, plus many interesting things that a man has to deal with.

Loss of identity is one of them.

Almost over night a new circle of friends arrives, maybe some old ones, with the common linkage of kids, a sort of collective misery. Oops, sorry, I mean mutual support system.

When this happens a man will become "Someone's Dad." Possibly even take on multiple personalities, one for each child. Men may in the eyes of some of their former friends retain a formal title of say Mr. or even get to hear your own name once in a while. Men may also occasionally come into contact with a few long term friends that remember who they were. But for several years a man will have the label of being someone's DAD. Coupled with this change of identity our activities change. You not only collect a different label you also will do completely different things.

Fortunately, for many men, they have had the basic training having been a child at least once. It is not unusual for some men to have kept some of this childish training up well into later life. Here you are a grown up man maybe with huge work responsibilities and you are sitting on a beach filling a tin can with sand turning it upside down and pretending that it is a castle.

These simple tasks can make you a super hero in the eyes of a child for a few years and in the eyes of this young person, almost a god. If only all of life was that simple. Enjoy it. For this phase will not last. It does however provide a man with the opportunity to regress to some primitive childhood behavior that being with this little person validates you to do.

Sitting on a beach on a nice day without a care in the world building sand castles, watching the sea come in and wash them away can be very relaxing and therapeutic. Unfortunately, you need to be with a child to get away with it. It is a fine line between being a great dad, and some silly guy sitting alone on the beach building sand castles.

I admit there have been times I have been quite involved in some mindless activity with one of my children and enjoying it, then having to face the disappointment of having to leave it because the child is bored. Maybe we should start a business called "Rent a Kid" to enable men to do childlike things without appearing to be a complete nut case.

MONTHLY VISITOR

I was not entirely sure where to put this in the book as it is such an important subject and can have a huge impact on a man. Understanding the monthly cycle of a woman should be a compulsory class for all boys from the age 11 through to 16. So much to learn and guess what? Just as you think that you have got it all worked out it will change. The monthly cycle has two phases that particularly interest the man. A lovely time just prior to the actual period where the woman may exhibit some very unusual behavior. This is often referred to as PMT (Pre Menstrual Tension) or PMS (Pre Menstrual Stress).

PMS can effect women in different ways. For most women their behavior for a few days may become irrational and they will maybe pick a fight and they could become a total nightmare to live with. This can often be accompanied with stomach pains and other bodily issues like fatigue or headaches. On the other hand some women may experience virtually nothing and maybe experience a heightened sex drive. These behavioral changes may go on until the actual period arrives.

The actual period may last a few days. The arrival of the oral contraception (the pill) has done a lot to control this time and maybe reduce some of the PMT symptoms.

During this time sex may be off limits depending upon the women. Some have no problem just carrying on, most prefer not to. So worst case scenario for a man is to have a lengthy and traumatic period of PMT coupled with the "Period" when the women may not be interested in sex.

At the extreme this could mean that a man could not have his lovely partner available for his number one pastime for over 12 days every 28 days. Maybe a man should test drive a prospective woman for a few months to see how their cycle is affecting them and to see what he is dealing with, as all women are different. Just a word of caution, women are much better than men at suffering in silence and without complaint so they may mask what they are really feeling in this getting to know you time. (Be lucky if that gets past the editorial team.)

As with all visitors, sometimes they are welcome, sometimes they are not. During those early years the monthly visitor will act as a major motivation for men, who worry about a pregnancy, to understand the joys of the monthly cycle. Many an hour being spent researching to see if this late period is the sign of an unwanted guest or just the randomness of the cycle.

Chocolate can be a very useful indicator to warn a man of those tricky few days before the monthly visitor arrives. Irrational and illogical behavior may be present but an increase in chocolate intake could warn the thinking man to keep out of the way during this danger period. It may even act as a palliative to get the women through it. A wise and caring man with an instinct for self preservation would maybe have a few bars of chocolate available "just in case."

When these monthly periods stop it is usually because of pregnancy or the "Change." Both of these events can trigger an over consumption of chocolate.

Another potentially disturbing fact is that the monthly visitor is starting much earlier in America. Some girls under the age of 10 are starting their periods and developing as women sooner. The informed opinion is putting this down to all the hormones that we are eating in our diet that get fed into our food chain. No specific research has been done to support this opinion but comparative checks in countries with a more basic, often very poor, diet has not indicated the same trends.

These monthly visitors can be very challenging for any man that has to deal with women. Either in personal relationships, maybe at work or even just dealing with women in the normal goings on in life. You may get to see three or four different women all in the same body every month. What joy. I appreciate that some women may see this as a huge and debilitating thing to deal with every month and I have some sympathy.

Let me put a positive view. If a women does something totally irrational or out of character the expression "time of the month" can be used to excuse a multitude of sins. Men have no such equivalent cop out to explain occasional bad behavior.

ALL CHANGE

Menopause is a term used to describe the permanent cessation of the primary functions of the human ovaries: the ripening and release of ova and the release of hormones that cause both the creation of the uterine lining and the subsequent shedding of the uterine lining (a.k.a. the menses or the period). Menopause typically (but not always) occurs in women in midlife during their late 40's or early 50's, and signals the end of the fertile phase of a woman's life.

That is put quite clinically and in a very straight forward way is what the Menopause. (Or "Change" is all about.)

If only life was that simple.

Women are all different of course and they react differently to this hormonal change in their life.. Some breeze through the change without any problems or any consequence at all. They come out rampant, full of energy, and without the risk of a pregnancy. Great, you must be out there some-where? (Editors comment. "Yes millions of us.")

We should, however, deal with the worst case scenario then anything less will be a pleasant upside. Hot flushes, irrational behavior, tearful epi-sodes for no apparent reason, well not to our simple logical male minds. But these woman are experiencing a major hormonal and emotional event, moving away from being able to have children.

For some women this can go on for 10 years or more and be very depressing. They may have major personality changes and relationships fail. Modern medicine of course can offer some relief for the more extreme effects. One woman told me that these effects have been going on for over 20 years and when she asked the doctor when they would end he replied "Maybe never!"

This is not only hormonal but emotional. You could have a completely different person to deal with. This could be temporary or short term. If you are really lucky the woman will breeze through it, take some hormone therapy and become rampant sex monsters. I put this sentence in to provide optimism and encouragement. You never know what is going to happen.

Reproduction "Russian Roulette" is also pretty dangerous game to play during this period, as the periods, stop, start and can be missed, maybe go a few months then another one. Guess what? In the middle of all this change period you may get another major surprise. A baby.

What a joy, just as you were getting used to life without all those little screaming kids around. Maybe the good news is that your other children are now old enough to be a bit more helpful.

Modern medical developments have been quite active in this area and can provide some interesting drugs to minimize the impact of this change. HRT (Hormone replacement therapy) for example. The impact of these drugs can not only eliminate the worst side effects of the change they may create a wonderful highly sexually charged woman who has no risk of pregnancy. It happens.

WHO IS THIS WOMAN?

In my experience women are much more capable of change than us simple men. Women play many different roles much better. Daughter, Mother, Lover, New Woman, Worker, Grandmother, etc. Women seem to move more effortlessly between roles than men do in their different roles. Women often deal with several roles all at the same time. The male often "single dimensional being" sometimes struggles to cope with being a multi-dimensional person.

One of the relatively recent phases of modern life is the emergence of "New Woman" in their middle years. This could happen when they are round the age of 40, give or take a few years. Children maybe away from home and they are comfortable in themselves as women. Maybe they are financially independent, looking for "More from Life." They realize they may have several decades left to do their own thing. Good luck to them, I think this is great.

However for a man, it can be a seriously threatening and intimidating shock and horror. He may have to compete for this woman's affections on an equal level and not rely on the adulation because he is "The Man" or "The bread winner" or because he can provide shelter and support. Many of the things that a man has relied on to keep the woman content may have gone. She will either downgrade their importance or she will be able to do them for herself, often much better. Independent woman is born.

During this period a "New Woman" has certain expectations and maybe a change of priorities. They want a better quality of emotional relationship and better sex. They enjoy their friends more, they start to look after themselves better and they start to value different things.

They may also want to develop a life of their own as recognition for what they believe to have been their sacrifices of the earlier years. For example putting their children before a career, or putting up with an unsatisfactory personal relationship for the sake of family unit. So the kids have gone.

Men have to be careful as they could be gone as well?

WHERE DID SHE GO?

This new woman may have dumped you? It happens. One of the growing areas of divorce is between couples who have been together a longtime, children have left home, they feel fit, healthy, invigorated and realize that maybe they are not compatible any more.

Guess who usually pulls the trigger. The woman!

Second guess, who may be paying for this new life. You!

Woman are cute, they can adjust to change quickly and are more focused on getting what they want. It is all the training women receive when they were bringing the children up and running the home and maybe holding down a job. They have spent years on the treadmill just to keep everything in place. Including usually a man.

As an interesting observation on why couples split up is that women tend to leave a relationship because they want to get out. A man tends to leave a relationship if he is offered what he believes to be a better life, typically with another woman.

If a man does not put enough in the bank during the hard times, and support the woman, you are maybe gone. The timing can be really bad for a lot of men. Just as they are starting to wind down and enjoy life. Maybe planning to spend more time at home relaxing etc., and by implication they expect this woman to look after them. It is not to be. Some men will have to deal with maybe a couple of really traumatic situations. A divorce with a serious loss of wealth plus having to adjust to the world of being single and actually having to cook, clean and look after themselves. For many men this will be double "whammy" on the scale of trauma.

DOMESTIC HELL

I remember a friend telling the story of when he was really busy earning a fortune to keep his wife and kids in the manner to which they had become accustomed. He frequently worked late. One night he came home to find everyone in bed with a note on the kitchen table "Your dinner is in the dog."

Many men are just not programmed to look after themselves. Simple tasks like cooking, cleaning, and laundry are just beyond them. So if we are unfortunate to have this "New Woman" get up and go, the man could be left with domestic hell. Even if the woman does not leave you permanently, she will quite often want more freedom and this may not always include you.

Remember the progression. You, children, friends, chocolate.

This will be the friends phase which is really about the woman finding herself. "The Big Challenge" for the man is to step up and become one of those friends for the "New Woman." She will want to get out and do things. Being a domestic slave to you probably did not make the cut on her new list of priorities. Men, be prepared and get some skills in the domestic arena. Eating out all the time is expensive and not always healthy. Chefs love sugar, fat, cream, cheese, butter and salt, unfortunately your body doesn't.

Men should understand how a home works. I do not count the fact that you may have been throwing a lump of meat on a barbecue for years and swigging beer. This is not cooking and does not count, especially if you do not do all the cleaning up afterwards.

No.

Here we may be wandering into some difficult territory so first to get out of the way I have absolutely no sympathy or support for any man that uses violence against a woman, whether physical, verbal or sexual. It shows no class and they deserve everything bad that may come to them.

But one of the slogans that is used by people who are active in the various excellent movements that try and protect women and give them more rights is the term "No means No!"

This is the problem. For the vast majority of us regular men in a normal relationship dealing with a woman, we know that "No" does not always mean "No." Quite frequently it means "Maybe" if you ask again nicely. It may mean "Yes" but I am not the sort of person that should be saying yes. In fact quite often women will say No as a way of really saying yes. One of those "Feminine Wiles."

Men can never be certain that "No" means "No" because usually they lack perception and empathy. A man may not fully realize that "No" did actually mean "No" until out of the situation and all alone, or talking to a police officer.

WOMEN IN THE WORK PLACE

The increasing role of women in the work place is a major advantage to any organization and a boost to the economy. They bring a balance and maturity that men frequently lack. With their multi-tasking skills and strong work ethic anywhere they work will be enriched by their presence. (This paragraph is under strong editorial control!)

The reality is that woman have the same work profile and ability mix as men. Some are ambitious and driven and some just see work as a job. Some are talented and able. Some are just average and doing the job. So let,s get into trouble and pass a few opinions from some personal observations on women in the work place.

Usually they work harder and are more focused.

They have a better multi-tasking capability as they often have a home and family to look after.

They have more insecurities but are usually better than they realize.

The female equivalent of the alpha male can be ruthless and totally driven.

They use feminine wiles, yet complain if they are criticized for it.

They are more objective and pragmatic than most men.

They sneak away and eat chocolate hidden in their purse, desk, filing cabinet or anywhere. One of the women in the research group, a lawyer based in London, said her office had a whole filing cabinet drawer with "emergency chocolate."

THE GIRL FRIENDS

A short while back I read a very interesting article about how some woman prefer the company of their friends than sex. Apparently a lively animated conversation between close girlfriends releases a load of brain stimulating chemicals that can be more powerful than an orgasm. Just imagine what would be happening if they were all having a chocolate desert at the same time. Men, we have absolutely no answer to that.

Women love their friends much more than men love their male friends. They have many more really close friends than most men do. A recent survey revealed that something like 60% of men do not have a really close friend that they would view as a confidant at the same level as would a woman.

LET'S GO TO BED

Language is a funny thing it means different things to different people and at different times in their life and in different contexts. Like the term "Restroom."

I have been in countless rest rooms and witnessed some very variable and occasionally unusual behavior. The one thing I have never seen yet is anyone "Resting?"

In dealing with women one term has so many meanings "Let,s go to Bed" or a similar one "Did they sleep together." Both of these terms in those early years are a euphemism for having sex.

The younger and more horny you are the less a bed and certainly sleep is a factor in the outcome. The term "Let,s go to Bed" means different things through out a woman's life.

The active words are frequently the "Let us" or "I am going." If a woman says I am going to bed this usually means, I am tired, going to sleep, do not disturb, do not wake, goodnight. In the middle years for the busy woman this may be her only sanctuary to escape. You being a part of that sanctuary is often not required.

If a woman says "Let us go to bed" well then choices arise. If you are hot and horny then go for it, enjoy. If she is hot and horny and your are not? Find something to do and hope that she falls asleep.

Treat your sex life like a sandwich. The early years, and maybe the later years, going to bed usually means for an interesting time. In those crazy busy middle years, for most women, it usually means to sleep.

HUNTED DOWN.

It has to be a woman that came up with the term "Cougar." The older woman hunting down the younger man. Biologically perfect, these older women are able to sap the strength out of the younger men. For the older man, wow, less work to do as these women can be very energetic. Good luck to all concerned.

Let me include in this section all men in their 50s or 60s or even 70s that find themselves on the singles market. If they have been in a long term relationship for several years, maybe having been dumped by new woman, this can be a terrifying period with some serious downsides.

At first it sounds fun, to have the whole world in front of you, well maybe. The emergence of internet dating and all these match making sites can present endless opportunities to meet all these highly sexually charged women that are frequently making up for lost time. This is especially true if the woman had married young with only a little sexual experience before she was married. This could be her time for doing the experimenting that she should maybe have done in her earlier years.

It is common to meet woman in this group who want some form of excitement after a long and unsatisfactory relationship. These woman can be uninhibited and adventurous, definitely a job for the younger man. Maybe?

A friend recently went through this experience. At first he thought this was great. He went on the internet and also replied to a few advertisements in the newspapers where he had to learn a whole new language. SWM, GSOH, NS, etc. Within a few weeks, he had dates with several woman and he was out 3 or 4 nights most weeks. Nice women all very sensible and looking for love. At this age, sex with mature experienced consenting adults, was usually fairly quick and adventurous .

His poor body which had been used to maybe once a month, if he was lucky, was now having to perform several times a week. I remember talking to him about this new life and he said that his main problem was that he had found new muscles in his arms and back that were now hurting badly. Within a few weeks he began to dread the next encounter and what may be expected of him. Remember that men peak physically for sex at 18 maybe 40 or 50 years ago.

The other thing that happened was that the juggling of the various women after a few weeks was becoming an emotional strain. He was talking like a double, or even triple dating teenager with all the attendant problems, jealousies and dramas. Woman who started off saying they wanted a "no strings attached good time with nothing serious!" Right! Were now giving him a hard time because he wanted to go and play golf on a Saturday instead of coming round to do jobs on their houses. Most men are not programmed for this excitement in later life. He realized things had to change when he ended up having four meals in one day just to keep the three women in his life happy.

There is also an increasingly large group of elderly men that have opted out of wanting to find and enjoy a committed relationship with a woman. The reason is fairly straightforward, well to another man anyway. These men have a waning sex drive so there are no raging hormones driving them to mate. This generation are maybe from the old school and have older more chauvinistic and respectful values that may not be totally in tune with the requirements of "Modern Woman".

These older men probably have little experience as they were not as active with many partners as today's modern man. Lastly it is a lot of work to form a relationship with another, often demanding, woman. Their male mates provide a much more comfortable, less demanding, lifestyle.

These later years also have another more serious danger. STDs or sexually transmitted diseases which do not discriminate on age or sex. If the place is warm friendly and nurturing they will go there. One the highest growth rates for STDs is in this group. What happens is that many people have had a long term relationship without any protection, the threat of children has gone and the thought of using a condom, maybe for the first time in several years, is just too much. Plus, there as no classes showing these virile seniors how to put a condom on a banana. For most of them they would probably prefer to just eat the banana than go through all that again. A feeling of "this will not happen to me" is common in this group of sexually charged people often making up for lost time. The public health people are really worried about this trend as some hitherto STDs that had been on the decline are becoming much more evident.

A word about the "Little Blue Pill." A blessing by providing opportunities for sex when the mind is willing but the body requires some help. Maybe a curse as "New Woman" now has expectations and the pill may remove the excuses? Interestingly one of the largest markets for these pills is with young college kids experimenting and trying to offset the effects of alcohol.

A final thought about activity in this older group and the increasingly common large age differences in relationships. I read a comforting article about men and women marrying much younger partners. For the man marrying the younger woman it can extend the man's life expectancy, keeping him young, needing to stay fit etc. For the woman, marrying the younger man, the opposite is true as the social pressure and the need to stay attractive can be demanding. Absolutely no idea if this is true, but it makes sense.

To close this section about the older group of increasingly more sexually active people a comment from a man living in a retirement community.

"It is great here with all these horny women. None of them can get pregnant, yet most of the men look as though they are!"

I would, however, like to pay tribute to some really remarkable women in this group. These are the women that have got it all together. They have had many experiences that life can offer, pretty well-versed about men and what they can and cannot do. They have carved out their own path and achieved a good state of independence. They are often single and have many interests and do not need a man except on their terms, which can be very demanding. Quick sex is usually not on the agenda. These women are also far more capable than most men to survive on their own, taking from life and relationships what they require.

There are some very special women in this group and men should seek them out as friends and learn from them. They will certainly not put up with the usual male crap, except when they maybe want to. Usually for amusement.

ARRIVAL OF THE CHOCOLATE.

You are sitting with a beautiful woman talking about the state of the nation and the price of bread. Hoping that the conversation will move into something more positive. Then you mention chocolate.

Her eyes light up and she answers.

I have a piece every day when I wake up, it is full of great stuff and keeps me slim. After the last bite has gone it feels like "A party in my mouth."

How can any man compete with that?

WHEN DOES CHOCOLATE FIRST ENTER A WOMAN'S LIFE.

One of the research women confirmed the point mentioned earlier about the effect of chocolate if taken by women when they are pregnant or breast feeding. She believed that when her mother was carrying her in the womb she ate a lot of chocolate and consequently gave birth to a daughter with an "in built" desire for chocolate.

It doesn't get any earlier than that. Well maybe chocolate flavored sperm. What a great business idea. The packaging could however be a problem, but the idea is good.

THE TASTING EXPERIENCE DEFINED

Women love chocolate and frequently eat it alone and often in secret. Chocolate however is best shared and the sharing is usually a better experience if you understand the six levels of the tasting expertise. The aim would be to develop your chocolate tasting skills through each stage to eventually achieve stage 6. The ultimate tasting experience.

Stage 1 is when just one person eats chocolate and achieves a feeling of deep satisfaction, which your tasting partner has yet to achieve.

Stage 2 is when the other partner, also alone, achieves the same feeling of deep satisfaction. Both people now understand and appreciate the value and taste of Chocolate.

Stage 3 represents a breakthrough as both you and your partner achieve that same feeling of satisfaction at the same time. A major achievement on the way to achieve stage 6.

Stage 4. Is when one of you achieves the same feeling of satisfaction as in the first 3 stages but also there is an added feeling that is so strong that it releases a powerful emotional response. This could be very moving, tears, maybe laughter but overall a deeper feeling of emotional satisfaction.

Stage 5. This is when the other partner also reaches this same deep feeling of satisfaction and experiences the same deep emotional experience. Both people have now experienced this higher level of satisfaction.

Stage 6. The ultimate sharing experience for sharing and tasting chocolate. This is when both tasters achieve this feeling of deep appreciation and emotional release at the same time. Maybe for the very advanced tasters a brief feeling of immortality. You both experience that wonderful moment of self appreciation that chocolate has brought you together to share this glorious moment of togetherness. At this level it is not about the chocolate.

These tasting skills are very difficult to achieve, most tasters can fairly easily achieve stages 1 and 2. Stage 3 can be difficult and takes training and practice. Stages 4, 5 and 6 are not really about the chocolate, This is when you realize that your tasting partner has the same values and appreciations as you and that you bond using your shared appreciation of chocolate. This is usually wonderful. Very few tasters reach these higher stages.

To find a taster with the same understanding of chocolate as yourself and to have a deep emotional connection is rare. Even these rare beings sometimes just want the quick fix of a chocolate bar.

There can be no guarantees with the tasting experience.

WHY WOMEN LIKE
CHOCOLATE

When I was doing the research I asked most of the women "Why chocolate, what is so special about it?" These are some of the comments that I received;

It never lets you down.

I can get it anytime anywhere I like.

It will always like me.

It tastes smooth and silky.

It is like having a party in my mouth.

It gives me a high when depressed,

I just take a couple of pieces and it makes me feel great.

It has a lot of great stuff in it and gives me a high.

It has to be the right chocolate, not this milky stuff full of fat and sugar.

I can get it when I want on my terms, and eat it when ever I need to.

Chocolate never disappoints like men do. So many romantic films out there that men are just not able to match up to.

It helps me slim. The theory from this woman is as follows. She keeps two large bags of chocolate buttons in the fridge but still buys and eats other chocolate. Every day she looks at the untouched bags of chocolate buttons and feels good that she has the will power not to eat them.

It makes me feel independent. If a man buys me a box of chocolates I would probably not eat many of them. The box will include all the bad stuff and not the dark good stuff that I need!

Some women seemed to equate chocolate not only with pleasure but also independence and control. Three powerful factors for everyone.

65% of the women interviewed preferred chocolate to sex.

FLOWERS V CHOCOLATE.

The Greeks considered flowers to be very important and associated them with the gods. Flowers for hundreds of years have been used to show affection and emotions to another person.

The one use of flowers that I thought was interesting was the bridal bouquet. In medieval times in England personal hygiene was some what lacking. In some families a bath was taken very infrequently, with the same water, and in sequence with the man first and poor baby last. This led to the expression "Do not throw the baby out with the bath water." The water at the end of the sequence was very murky and muddy. In these some what smelly times the idea was that the bride would carry flowers to hopefully mask the smell.

Flowers are always a great idea and women love them, they especially love the ideas behind them. But flowers do not give them a fix. They are transitionary which is an interesting point because a bunch of flowers may well last longer than a bar of chocolate. Flowers are however very safe as they represent a straight forward statement of intent with no underlying control issues. Of course, both win the day.

SEX

A word of caution about this section. The nature of the subject,
which is very personal, inherently makes some of the information suspect.
Many people will not talk about sex and relationships. Those that
do talk about sex are prone to understate or exaggerate.

Nearly all of the surveys that I have looked at and taken the
information from used a very small sample of people.

Consequently everything you read in this section has to be
taken with a large degree of caution and circumspect.

SEX.

Here I have done some research, mainly desk based which was great fun! But not as much field work as I would have liked. Dam this climate change. Before I launch in to some of the research that I have found and listened to over the years a couple of basic points.

Allegedly, when discussing sex (and many people will not) you have to roughly divide what men say by a factor of three but multiply what women say by a factor of three. In simple terms if a man says he has had fifteen partners its five and if a women says five it's fifteen. Get the picture. So if most people will not talk about it and there is such a wide disparity between what men and woman say how do we look at any research sensibly. The answer, of course, is that it is a fascinating subject and we instinctively compare what we hear and read to our own experiences. As always with most aspects of human behavior.

The other point to make is that if you believe the information that is available, we are sexually active for an average of 40 years. Have sex 2.8 times a week and it lasts approx. ten minutes, that's if you are in Europe, the Americans being much more efficient can typically be done in eight minutes. A huge 20% improvement in productivity. Well done America.

If we then take these highly suspect and dubious statistics and apply them to the average life expectancy of eighty five years then we spend less than one tenth of one percent of our life having sex. Which is nothing. Well so I have been told!

Therefore, how come then it is so important that we men apparently think about it several times a day? How come it is features in so many walks of life, media, advertising, movies. Books.

Having got those two fundamental points out the way let us talk about some of the research that I have read or heard over the years.

If a man was offered sex by a hundred women at random how many offers would he take up just on how they look. Answer, 95%. If a woman was given the same offers with a hundred men. Answer, 3%. Clue there men! I think this piece of information is also interesting from the perspective of who controls when sex takes place, which I think is usually the woman. Look at the odds, if a woman decides to go out and have a good time she has a 95% chance of success if a man goes out with the same intention he will have a 3% chance of success. The logic is a real stretch but even with a deep discount on the percentages I think the point is valid.

Why do women have sex or as Sigmund Freud called it "The great question?"

I was listening to a radio program that indicated that when a woman has sex she really only wants to 40% of the time. The rest of the time it is typically for a quiet life or because it is easier to say yes than to keep saying no. Some interesting reasons were mentioned for why women just go along with having sex;

For a quiet life. (84% women say they have done that)
So that he falls asleep and I can do my own thing.
To get a job done round the house.
To get control of the remote control for the TV.
My favorite. To get him to take the trash can out.
Sympathy.
Boredom.

Men, does it bother you that when having sex that approx. 60% of the time the woman does not really want to? Most of the time they are just doing it because you just want the pleasure. I do not really want to know the answer because I think that I know it already. Women have sex for romantic reasons, like in the movies, less than 10% of the time. Depressing for you romantics.

In a serious long term relationship sex is usually very important but it is different for the sexes. For men they have to have sex to feel loved. For woman they have to feel loved to have sex. As Shakespeare would say, "Therein lies the rub?" Which apparently for most men is unfortunately how they spend a lot of their time.

If you ladies are unhappy because a man immediately falls asleep after sex this is what is to blame; Norepinephrine, serotonin, oxytocin, vasopressin, nitric oxide (NO), and the hormone prolactin. This is the cocktail of stuff that the male brain (Not an oxymoron, behave!) releases that send men to sleep. The good news is that if men are deficient in prolactin then they are able to recover faster.

What these simple facts mean is that men are programmed perfectly for sex. A man hunts, conquers, copulates and ejaculates and then the brain releases a whole bunch of cocktails to send a man into a blissful sleep. Perfect!

Oh no such luck!

That wonderful moment of completion is exactly when the questions start.

Do you really love me?
Why are going to sleep?
Will you cuddle me?
Do you only want me for sex?

During this critical post copulation period a deep struggle may be going on inside a man's head. Half of the brain is trying to get into idyllic sleep. The other half of the brain is trying to stay awake and focus on these questions. There is enough consciousness to realize that if you get one of these answers wrong you are "Screwed." Or even worse not screwed ever again. Well not by this particular woman or maybe not by her for a longtime. It happens.

This post-coital period is a serious danger period for men as they may be basking in that wonderful after glow of soporific contentment but also having to walk a tight role with the mouth. One slip could be disastrous and snoring in the middle of a meaningful discussion is not normally a good idea.

To put the other side of the argument. This post coital moment can be a moment of great joy. This brief few seconds after the physical release is when a man may realize that they are happy to be here with this great and wonderful woman. The urgency of the testosterone fueled chase is out the way and they may actually look at the woman as a real person, and carry out a very quick evaluation as to if that was really such a good idea. Ladies be aware that in the evolution of a relationship this is a critical time and can last just a few seconds. Especially the very first time.

Men are biologically programmed wrong as well, they reach a physical peak sexually at around eighteen, where as women reach their sexual peek in their late thirties, and many of them keep on climbing! What sort of deal is that for men. Some one up there clearly got that wrong? Just when a man finds out what it is all about his body is not able to reach its full operating efficiency. They say "Life is wasted on the young" which is so true in this situation.

A few other good pieces of research are as follows; if you think everyone else is having a better sex life than you, they are usually not. If a relationship starts with hot and horny sex then statistically the less likely it is that the relationship will last. Too much sex or sex too early in a relationship is not necessarily a good thing it increases the probability of the relationship failing. Mind you, I did read the small print and the difference is very small, so to the male brain probably not significant.

The main reason this chapter on SEX is in the book is to explain that sex is not of primary importance for woman. For 60% of the time women have sex when they would prefer not to. That is the reason this chapter is in the book and why this chapter is so long.

This chapter has nothing to do with the fact that SEX sells and that many of you will have picked up the book browsed across this section and decided to buy the book. If you are one of them, thank you sir, as you will probably be a man. Or will you?

ADVICE TO WOMEN
(ABOUT MEN)

We are different, we are different, we are different. Women usually need to be told things three times before it registers? Oops, did that get past the editors! Being different is maybe the bad news.

The good news is that we are very simple and basic creatures, we are nowhere near as complex as a woman. In fact, no where near as complex as a woman may believe that we are. So do not waste all that energy and emotional drama trying to understand something that is not there to understand, "The complexity of a man."

Women you give us far too much credit for so much. Sex, constant praise and a shiny toy to play with normally does it for most men.

This does not apply to me, of course, I am a caring, emotionally mature literary genius. This brings me to my next point.

We can often be delusional about ourselves. Women please humor us and make allowances. It is much easier in the long run than constantly criticizing and trying to bring us down to earth. A small example occurred whilst writing this book. In a previous existence I worked in industry and this writing is a whole new experience for me. Getting carried away a little I mentioned to this woman friend who knows me very well that I may start calling myself a writer. She replied, make sure that you spell it right! Totally uncalled for.

Men like to go away and hide, talking things through doesn't work for us the same way as it does for you. Severe emotional trauma, especially in a relationship will typically spark isolation and thought. Men talking to each other may be a temporary distraction but it is often limited to getting drunk and finding another woman. Plus the usual unhelpful bits of advice, "Treat them mean it keeps them keen," "Just wait she will realize what she is missing," "You are lucky to be out of that," "That was a close one," "Women!"

This may all be therapeutically bonding for some men but it is somewhat lacking in emotional empathy. No caring questions like "How are you feeling?" "Would you like to talk to me about it?" "Have you talked to her and explained how you are feeling?"

Men require constant reassurance that you love us and think that we are wonderful. Think of us as children, it will help. Women have a much more advanced emotional coping system than men. You can use it to do all sort of things that men are unable to do. Multi-task, share your affections with children and girl-friends and of course enjoy "chocolate."

One of the women who I met was quite chatty and she had been married for several years and allegedly had a very hot sex life and a very happy husband. She said she does not get all this moaning that women do about men and always wanting sex. In her view, sex should be like food, sometimes you may want a quick snack and the couple of minutes!! that it takes should be just done and got out of the way, as it is easier in the long run than to keep saying no. Maybe once a week a proper meal together, by appointment. Then once a month or so a full gourmet feast to be looked forward to. I pass this advice on from another woman without comment. Which is very difficult, trust me.

A little bit of advice, in your crazy multi-tasking "saving the world" day, and I say that sincerely because I think as the master race you are usually the person that makes most relationships work. You are far more capable than us one dimensional men at keeping everything in place. I sincerely mean that.

Set an alarm on one of your many gadgets for a certain time each day. When the alarm goes take a few minutes to do some thing nice for the man in your life to let him know that you love him and that he is special. A few minutes every day will work wonders. To be entirely pragmatic this little gesture will save you loads of hours down stream having to deal with all the millions of questions that come out of our deep routed feelings of insecurity.

Men watch movies. This for many of us is our only reference point as to how to relate to women. We are not cute enough to learn by watching other people's behavior and we certainly don't talk about it to other men, like you do to other women. We also tend to wander into these long term relationships and then wake up and realize we are in one. Women on the other hand seem to have all these things planned and programmed into you from an early age. So many women have thought about their wedding day, the children that they will have, the type of home etc etc. Without ever having met a man that could maybe make that possible. I do not know a single man that ever thinks like this, well not without being ridiculed.

Men usually have no relationship plans, we have not thought any of it through, we just react to what you would like us to do. Therefore we have to rely on Hollywood to educate us.

The good news is that we know that women like the "Grand Gesture." Proposing in public and all those wonderful moments. These high spots can of course create a life time magical memory. The bad news is that we think we are done after that. Where as women realize that it has only just begun and this where the work of building a relationship really starts.

We are also not "telepathic," you have to help us, when you are upset. When we have done something really stupid and insensitive talk to us. The long meaningful silence does not help. If we are inexperienced and stupid we will make the mistake of asking you what we have done. ("We always assume it is our fault by the way, we should get brownie points for that".) This simple question usually leads to you giving us a really bad time, we get reminded of all our faults and the minor or not so minor mistakes that we made in the past, like not picking the paint can up when we were working on "Noah's ark." This can go on and on and on and on. If on the other hand we are reasonably smart we may just leave you alone for a while, be nice and hope that what ever is causing you to behave this way goes away. Which it quite often will. You are so busy that events may over-take you.

If we are super smart we will figure out something is wrong, maybe work out what it was and then *do something really nice that replaces those nasty thoughts in your head.* Now here is the issue, do not wait too long for this to happen as a disappointment can be crushing. The thinking goes something like this. When, and if, *we reach that "Nirvana" state of being able to understand what makes a woman tick and how to do something nice to deal with your mood,* the catch 22 is that if we are that cute then our actions would never put you in that mood in the first place.

ADVICE TO MEN

Understand that if you enter a long term relationship your life will never be the same again. Better or worse? Up to you and the luck of the draw.

Read the book " The Second Sex" by Simone de Beauvoir. Treat it as a text book and learn. In particular memorize the phrase "Love to a man is a thing apart, for a woman it is her total existence." Mention this phrase and your understanding of it in conversation with women. Be careful it could be dangerous as the woman may briefly think that you are a caring sensitive soul.

Little things mean a lot. That thoughtful gesture, the non threatening gentle touch as you pass. This is important. Size does not count.

If you are a powerful man understand the difference between "Power" and "Control." Women may love power but they will hate being controlled.

Treat your hands as your best friend. Learn to touch a woman gently, sensuously and in a caring non threatening way. If you get this wrong your hands may well be your only friend.

Editorial input. Learn how to kiss a woman properly. A woman can give herself a nice orgasm but cannot give herself a meaningful kiss.

Learn some domestic skills for two reasons. Just in case you have to, if dumped? Or to win massive brownie points by cooking the odd meal or doing the laundry once in a while. This gesture will usually receive an exceptionally appreciative response! Maybe those tactics of screwing up simple jobs the first time you were asked to do in the hope of avoiding being asked again was not such a good idea.

Listen, Listen, Listen. The three times rule applies to men as well. Sorry to have to admit it. Or if this is too much to learn, then pretend to listen.

I was recently listening to a well known woman in public life explaining why her marriage was so good. She said that her husband was great, he provided the security and support that resulted in her success. She consequently always felt confident and supported when she was developing new and exciting areas for herself. Would your partner say this about you? Or are you a control freak that resents your partners success? If you are the later, the clock is ticking as new woman will emerge at some point.

Do not try to "Fix Things." Women do not like being fixed. It is an impossible task anyway. They will usually always get there themselves and depressingly quicker and better than a man would.

Understand the 90/10 rule. Foreplay 90% Sex 10% not the other way round.

Accept that you will always be wrong. Sometimes you will need to have this explained to you. Listen carefully and do not disagree or argue. This will prolong the pain and reinforce the memory. Apologize quickly and sincerely, it will save time.

BUY CHOCOLATE, LOTS OF CHOCOLATE.

I may have to re think this last point.
See the conclusions later on in the research section.

CHOCOLATE OR SEX

You asked that I should choose.
Sex can sometimes be grand
But chocolate removes the blues.
Chocolate can be planned
Sex depends upon who is on hand
Chocolate makes me feel so good
Usually better than a man could
So if I have to choose
What about my shoes?

RESEARCH FINDINGS

The next few pages contain the detailed interviews and research
carried out in the USA and UK. 61 women were spoken to.
An unexpected learning journey.

Men, prepare to be depressed.

This research was carried out in the USA and the UK by approaching women, nearly all of them at random and in public places. The women were all ages and from different social groups and had differing status. I first asked them if they would like to help on some research for a book. If they agreed I then asked them if they liked chocolate which only one woman out of 61 said no. Most women looked at me as if I was a touch stupid for asking such an obvious question. Several women said, "What women does not like chocolate?"

I then asked if anything that I asked them may offend them, If they replied, no, then I outlined what I wanted to do;

Ask them one question to which they had to give an immediate reply without thinking.

The question being.

Que 1. Do you prefer sex or chocolate?

I noted the answers without comment. I then told them what the book was about and asked them two further questions, to which they could give a considered reply.

Que 2. Why do you think men have a hard time understanding women?

Que 3. What one piece of advice would you give to a man on how to relate to women better?

SUMMARY OF THE RESULTS

Number of women interviewed. 61

Number that preferred Chocolate to SEX. 35. (65%)

The answers were broadly the same in the USA and the UK at 65%.

The most common answer to question 2 was that men do not listen to women properly.

Therefore, not surprisingly the most common answer to question 3 was that men need to listen more.

The detailed answers and comments are in the next few pages.

USA RESEARCH

Most common answer. 14 different women all ages / Experiences.

    Que 1. Chocolate.

    Que 2. Do not listen.

    Que 3. Listen (and communicate).

Woman 50 plus, divorced, experienced currently not in a long term relationship.

    Que 1. Can I have both. Preferably at the same time.

    Que 2. We are just too complicated.

    Que 3. Engage brain before opening mouth.

30 Year old woman married less than one year.

    Que 1. Chocolate, and that is so true..

    Que 2. Not understand complexities of women.

    Que 3. Be thoughtful and patient.

Professional woman in her 30's Single.

    Que 1. Tough. But sex.

    Que 2. Think with the wrong head.

    Que 3. Need to be in touch with their feminine side.

Woman server in a restaurant in 40's was married now separated.

    Que 1. Oh my god do I have to chose. Sex.

        I can get chocolate any time.

    Que 2. Our moods.

    Que 3. Understand that we are in control.

Young lady in mid 20's Single. Shop manager.

    Que 1. Is this a trick question?

    Que 2. Need to listen.

    Que 3. Listen without intentions.

Woman married grown up children.

> Que 1. Both please.
>
> Que 2. We are always changing. They do not get that.
>
> Que 3. Be brave enough to be yourself.

Two married women out walking.

> Que 1. Sex, but its close. I have had some very good chocolate.
>
> Que 2. We are complex creatures.
>
> Que 3. Treat us like a "Goddess."

Woman late 50s single very experienced.

> Que 1. Oh my god. Sex.
>
> Que 2. Woman do not let men know their true feelings.
>
> Que 3. Just say yes. Its easier in the long run.

Woman late 30s divorced young child.

> Que 1. Sex.
>
> Que 2. They are just stupid.
>
> Que 3. Listen.

Woman in 50s recently divorced.

> Que 1. Chocolate. I know it will like me afterwards.
>
> Que 2. We are a lot more complicated.
>
> Que 3. Listen and be empathetic. Not try and fix things.

Woman 70 married 4 times well travelled woman of the world.

> Que 1. Not choosing. I deserve both.
>
> Que 2. Most men are too self absorbed to understand us.
>
> Que 3. Listen more, control less.

Two nurses in a top medical clinic.

> Que 1. Chocolate. Chocolate.

> Que 2. Do not listen. Plus we are more complex.

> Que 3. Listen. Not just pretend to listen.

Two more nurses in a top medical clinic.

> Que 1. Difficult. Probably sex but it would depend on the day.

> Que 2. Shopping. Men just do not get it.

> Que 3. Ask us, listen, do not keeping asking us again.

Shuttle driver at airport.

> Que 1. Sorry do not like chocolate. (Only 1 out of 61)

Shop assistant, young, very attractive, single.

> Que 1. Chocolate. It never disappoints you.

> Que 2. We just live in two different worlds.

> Que 3. Listen.

Graphic designer. Married young child.

> Que 1. Depends how tired I am. But chocolate.

> Que 2. Not understand that we tend to over think things.

> Que 3. Listen, or at least pretend to.

Graphic Designer.

> Que 1. Sex.

> Que 2. Not able to read us.

> Que 3. Buy loads of chocolate.

Restaurant worker. Married.

> Que 1. Chocolate.

> Que 2. Our emotions.

> Que 3. Be more respectful.

MALE SEX THERAPIST.

An interesting discussion with someone whom I met by chance in a Sedona coffee shop where we discussed some of my findings for this book. His first reaction was.

"Your are telling me, what with the chocolate and all their "Toys" men do not stand a chance unless there is some emotional connection."

(editorial comment. "That's how it should be")

We started to talk about this subject and I explained my surprise at two things; The high percentage of women that said that they preferred Chocolate to SEX. With such a small sample it was difficult to detect a trend but it did appear that the younger, more attractive and single women did seem to prefer chocolate more than the older more mature women.

His comments were interesting and I just repeat them for your consideration.

He said that even in these enlightened time of higher sexual awareness many woman did not fully understand about basic sexuality and in particular the female organism. He explained the answers that I had been receiving about women preferring chocolate by saying that many women had not been "made love to properly?" He then went on to explain that in his experience there were three levels of orgasmic pleasure and most women, not all, can achieve level one, some achieve level two and very few even know about, or achieve, level three which he termed "Anointing the Prince."

A fascinating and very interesting discussion. Have fun with your thoughts.

UK RESEARCH

Most common answer. 8 different women all ages / Experiences.

    Que 1. Chocolate.

    Que 2. Do not listen.

    Que 3. Listen (and communicate).

Two Flight attendants on a long haul flight. Young and single.

    Que 1. Chocolate. Chocolate.

    Que 2. They do not get the way we change our mind.

    Que 3. Just treat us nice and buy us lots of nice presents.

School teacher. Young and single.

    Que 1. Chocolate.

    Que 2. Not understand how women can multi-task.

    Que 3. Become gay. Show feminine side.

Business Executive, married twice no children.

    Que 1. Chocolate.

    Que 2. Men do not get how important children are to a woman.

    Que 3. Listen and look at a woman's face for a reaction to what you say.

Two single women on a train.

    Que 1. Sex. But sometimes chocolate does it for me.

    Que 1. Sex. I can get chocolate any time.

    Que 2. Not good at picking up signals. We say one thing and mean something else.

    Que 2. Men are very simple we expect too much from them.

    Que 3. Just do as you are told. Watch for hidden signals! (Read that back and think. Men have to see whats not there)

    Que 3. Do not buy a large box of chocolates. Probably not the right thing.

Oil company sales Executive on Train. Single.

> Que 1. Sex.
>
> Que 2. Completely different.
>
> Que 3. Listen and communicate.

Charity worker single mature lady.

> Que 1. Chocolate.
>
> Que 2. Everything.
>
> Que 3. Communicate.

Professional single lady.

> Que 1. Thats not fair.
>
> Que 2. We are just totally different.
>
> Que 3. Pretend to listen.

Spiritual advisor / Life coach. Married.

> Que 1. Chocolate.
>
> Que 2. Not get our moods and emotions.
>
> Que 3. Be a best friend.

Coffee shop assistant, young and single.

> Que 1. Sex. I think but its close. I love chocolate.
>
> Que 2. We are much more emotional.
>
> Que 3. Listen and try to understand more.

Married. Mature lady.

> Que 1. Chocolate.
>
> Que 2. We do not appreciate them always having sex on the brain.
>
> Que 3. Listen.

Young single business executive and writer.

      Que 1. Sex.

      Que 2. We are different I belief that men are from "Mars." (Not the
           chocolate company!)

      Que 3. Listen.

Mature married lady, market trader.

      Que 1. Chocolate.

      Que 2. No idea.

      Que 3. Buy loads of chocolate.

This answer to the third question was unusual so I asked more. Her husband
has a bar of chocolate waiting for her every night when she returns home
from work. When she asked him why? He replied "Just in case." She said "Just
in case what" and he replied "Just in case." Pretty advanced male thinking in
action. To use a daily bar of chocolate as a contingency to cover all eventuali-
ties. She asked for his name address to be withheld "Just in case."

Airline Check in. Young attractive single lady.

      Que 1. Chocolate.

      Que 2. Not understand our emotions.

      Que 3. Buy chocolate.

Married lady 18 year old daughter. At airport on vacation.

      Que 1. I know that I should say SEX but its chocolate.

      Que 2. Our emotions.

      Que 3. Do not listen enough.

Two ladies from Denmark in a coffee shop.

      Both married with children.

      Que 1. Sex. We Danish are more evolved!

      Que 1. Sex.

      Que 2. You do not have time for all that.

      Que 3. Improved communication.

A SPURIOUS RESULT.

One of our editors, Beverley, went away for a weekend with some women. One evening she had a group of 10 women, age range 40s to 70s mixed status, most were single and looking (hunting? oops sorry) and she asked them the "Three questions" with some interesting results.

Nearly all of them opted for SEX to chocolate and the group spent some considerable time discussing the quality of their SEX lives and the various failings of the male species. They had high expectations of what they wanted from men and from SEX.

These results were not typical of the ones that I had experienced. Two major differences; A woman was asking the questions and secondly it was a group discussion. Even a basic study of psychology reveals that a "one on one" versus "group discussion," will give different results. Plus women discussing men without a man present, always scary and more sexual?

It could be that all of the women that told me that they preferred CHOCOLATE did so because they did not want to admit to a man that they preferred SEX. I think not, but maybe?

I decided not to include these women in the overall results. I think Beverley stumbled into a "Cougar pack" maybe on a strategy discussion weekend. Frightening that these packs get together to compare notes before they go out hunting again.

SOME CONCLUSIONS. MAYBE?

Given that most of the women that were asked said they preferred chocolate, how come few of them answered for que 3. "Buy me chocolate?" I was really intrigued by that. If this had been a man survey and they had been asked to chose between beer and sex (maybe the next book) several of them for sure would have answered to que 3. Keep beer in the fridge, or something similar.

This intrigued me so much that I took the advice of one of the women in the research group and "asked and listened." The answer was probably the most revealing thing that I learnt writing this book. She said;

"It is about control, we want to use the chocolate on our terms, when we want to and not to be obliged to anyone."

Not the answer that I expected. A woman equating a gift of chocolate to control, almost like not wanting the dependency of the chocolate pusher. I am still processing this thought!

When I wrote the advice to men section I put at the bottom " Buy Chocolate" maybe this is a really bad idea as it may look to the woman like a play for control by the man. Complex is just too simple a word for women. Buying their own chocolate clearly provides an important reference point of independence for many women.

The sample was quite small but there was no obvious correlation in any age group between preferring chocolate to sex. Before I started I expected the younger, single and very attractive women to mainly prefer sex but this was not the case. Some of the most positive supporters of chocolate came from this group. Some of the more positive supporters for sex came from women in their 50's that were free uninhibited and maybe a bit scary! Some sounded really scary.

Another interesting point. Quite a few of the women after the discussion said "Do I get my chocolate now?" regardless of how they answered que 1. None of them said do I get my SEX now. Only a man would, of course, think this.

The book has covered the many ages of women. It has explained the importance of chocolate to most woman and how it gives them pleasure, independence and total control. It has also explained that sex is not as important to "Most" woman as men would like to believe that it is.

For "Most" men, depressingly, the most important thing that they want from a woman is sex. Men typically have sex for pleasure but guess what? Most woman most of the time only do it for a quiet life.

Men it is not going to work if you think that you can get between a woman and her chocolate. A conclusion which my admittedly very small research sample totally backs up.

MEN
ALL IS NOT LOST!

This book can be a depressing read for men to realize that in many ways women prefer a block of chocolate to sex. I am sure that most men will not have been paying attention. It is the sex that they prefer to the chocolate not the man in their life. I did not ask the woman if they preferred their partner to chocolate. A completely different question.

Maybe, I was scared to hear the answer. Interestingly none of the many woman that I spoke to challenged the fact that I had automatically linked sex as the main comparison point in the relationship. In most of the discussions it was clear that the woman instinctively viewed sex as the top priority for a man.

As soon as the word chocolate was mentioned, that became the total focus of the conversation, with no challenge as to the context. Women, in some cases, became almost hypnotic, certainly eyes wide open and lit up for most of them when asked about chocolate.

A man may often define a relationship through its sexuality equating the woman's attitude to sex as the key factor. For some relationships this may well be true. In most relationships sex is of course important but not in the way that most men believe it to be.

Women usually want to define the relationship first with many other factors. Sex is not usually top of the woman's list. Indeed for most of the woman that were asked, sex comes out second to a piece of candy albeit that candy has some special properties.

If, however, the man works at getting the women to like him first, then that is different. The woman will normally appreciate the partnership and closeness much more than some gymnastics in the bedroom.

Here is the great point. This is not an "Either / OR." Choice. If the woman gets to like you as a person, a partner, a confident and friend then you get to share everything. The SEX for sure and if you are really lucky some of the chocolate. The paradox, the less you chase the sex and focus on the woman as a person and "Listen", the more sex you will probably get.

Try it. It works.

If that does not do it

Then become gay and you will get loads of lovely women friends.

p.s. "Do you like chocolate?" Is a great pick-up line.

GOLDEN YEARS
(MAKE SURE NOT RUST)

Men, let me define the golden years for you. It is when you have had enough experience of relationships with women, or that one special woman, that you realize two things. How wonderful a great woman can be. How fulfilling a relationship with a truly great woman is. These two ideals are linked with the development of your emotional depth and capacity.

You not only have to have an understanding of this possibility but you must also feel fit enough in body and mind to believe that you still have the total capacity as a man to make this super relationship happen. Rare but it happens.

Relationships for most thinking men, are the Holy Grail. We stumble and discover as we go along dealing with the many phases of life. Enjoying, enduring and learning from the many phases of our relationships with women.

In those golden years, we may realize all the things that we could have done better. Maybe, just maybe, we will have a chance to put all those experiences to good use and make a truly great woman happy. This should of course also be a deep and enriching experience for the man. This could be the reward, for all the many issues that you have faced in dealing with the different phases and moods of a woman that have resulted in you being a better and more caring man.

This could be the perfect relationship a utopian and very happy state. It will never be totally achieved as all relationships are work in progress and that's fine by me. Be aware of the possibility and grasp the opportunity if it arises.

Until that happy opportunity comes along, men stay occupied working on what you want to do in order to make your self interesting. Become someone that a great woman may want to spend time with. Maybe, once in a while, go and sit on a quiet beach somewhere watching the sun slip away with a drink in hand gently writing a book musing over this wonderful life and your personal journey. Feeling good that there is no pressure.

Young men if you have all this to come, please brace your selves it can be a tough ride. Of course, you will not take any notice of the points in this book as they will not apply to you. Your life will be different and special. Believe this if it helps. Always remember that we humans have to find out about "Stuff" through experience, the hard way.

A special word to those lucky few that have plotted a course through this mine field, and have, or have had, a long and happy relationship with that special woman. Enjoying the golden years. Well done, you beat the odds.

The book has a happy ending after all.
Well, for some of you.

A FINAL THOUGHT

One outstanding piece of advice for men is to make sure
that a woman always has the LAST WORD.

One of the ladies that took part in the research said
"Eating chocolate was like having a party in her mouth."

She came back to me and offered to write the last section of this book.

A request that I am more than happy to agree with.

The thoughts of "Anastasia" to complete the book.
Thank You.

What I simply meant so that there is no misunderstanding is that when I eat chocolate I do indeed have a party in my mouth. But that party for me is the bursting of the sugar molecules that dance and linger in my mouth hanging on to all of my salivary glands. Indeed the flavor of the party hangs on for some time.

But there is no comparison to making love to the right man, not just any man. The man makes you quiver at the very sight of him, the one who adores you and you him, the one you want to wake up with and spend all your waking moments with. One to share a quiet romantic dinner out, or maybe in your home. One to cuddle up to on the sofa and watch a movie or just share a bottle of wine or some champagne maybe with some cheese and fruit. One that you would want to take a walk and maybe share some conversation with sitting on the veranda on a beautiful summer evening. One, that when he is sick, you would want nothing more to take care of him. One that you would not mind getting wet with while taking a walk in the rain but laugh remembering the child that you once felt like when you loved walking in the rain and taking off your shoes to feel the water splashing on your feet, with water trickling down your face. One that every time that you make love is as exciting as that special first time.

One you would love to spend a weekend with or a lifetime with.

Please know that there are many good men out there. You water to bloom, and feed to nourish and grow. It applies to everything in life. Just think how wonderful life would be for so many woman if each one of us took these small measures and applied them to someone special, and suddenly watch the blossoming of your life and your love.

Chocolate is wonderful, especially melted and shared with a special man maybe accompanied by some whipped cream and spread all over his adoring face or his strong chest. Imagine that party with the sugar molecules bursting in your mouth but most important imagine whom you are sharing your party with.

Parties take planning and are never the same. So why should your life not be the same.

Planning a new party creates thrill. Think of life as such.

No party is as great as that one with love.
Parties are always to be shared.
A party with chocolate alone is no fun.
A party with your someone special is an explosion.
A party with an anointed prince is very special.
An implosion and explosion all in one.
A real CHOCOLATE PARTY!!

Nothing is greater than
loving something wonderful
with someone wonderful.

OTHER BOOKS FROM MARCUS TEMPUS

To My Lover & Love Poems Book 2
Two books with a collection of original love poems written sensitively and evocatively to express deep and unconditional love. Either one would be an ideal gift to send to someone that you are deeply in love with and want to express that love in a more personal way. These two books will also appeal to someone that enjoys reading romantic poems.

To My Lover.
CreateSpace eStore: https://www.createspace.com/3906075

Love Poems. Book 2
CreateSpace eStore: https://www.createspace.com/3911243

Poems & Words Book 3
A collection of poems, words and short stories about life,
love, loss and people. Some are serious and some sad,
some observations on life and some are funny.
An eclectic mix of creative writing.

CreateSpace eStore: https://www.createspace.com/3938810

TO PURCHASE ADDITIONAL COPIES OF
"DO NOT GET BETWEEN A WOMAN AND HER CHOCOLATE"

If you have any thoughts about chocolate or
any related interesting experiences then please Email me.
I would love to hear about them.

marcustempus@hotmail.com

www.ingramcontent.com/pod-product-compliance
Lightning Source LLC
Chambersburg PA
CBHW070522030426

42337CB00016B/2069